Backyard Birding for Kids

An Introduction to Ornithology

Field Guide, Projects, and More!

Erika Zambello

Adventure Publications
Cambridge, Minnesota

ACKNOWLEDGMENTS

Thank you to my parents, who instilled in me a love of nature, and to my husband, who is always up for a new adventure.

DEDICATION

To Noah, my new favorite adventure partner.

Edited by Brett Ortler

Cover and book design by Jonathan Norberg

Proofread by Emily Beaumont

Front cover: **Black-Photogaphy/Shutterstock:** girl; **JGA/Shutterstock:** birdhouse; **Klahan/Shutterstock:** nest; and **Takahashi Photography/Shutterstock:** hummingbird.

Back cover: **JanyaSk/Shutterstock:** grass; **little birdie/Shutterstock:** feather; **mlorenz/Shutterstock:** owl; **Mystic Stock Photography/Shutterstock:** western tanager.

All photos copyright by their prospective photographers:
Sean Murphy: 136; and **Erika Zambello:** 119, 120.

credits continued on page 134

10 9 8 7 6 5 4 3 2
Backyard Birding for Kids
Copyright © 2022 by Erika Zambello
Published by Adventure Publications, an imprint of AdventureKEEN
310 Garfield Street South
Cambridge, Minnesota 55008
(800) 678-7006
www.adventurepublications.net
All rights reserved
Printed in China
ISBN 978-1-64755-223-7 (pbk.); ISBN 978-1-64755-224-4 (ebook)

Backyard Birding for Kids

An Introduction to Ornithology

Field Guide, Projects, and More!

Table of Contents

My Spark Bird

I started birding 10 years ago. My parents gave me a camera with a great zoom lens, and for the first time I could really see birds up close. One summer day, as I walked down a road in the Maine North Woods, I heard a buzzing call and noticed movement in the leaves overhead. Quickly raising my camera, I zoomed in on a tiny but colorful bird, busy looking for caterpillars on the tree's thinnest branches. After snapping a series of photos, I looked more carefully, and I suddenly knew he was the most beautiful bird I had ever seen. Blue on his back and head, the bird had bright white around his eyes and a flame-colored throat. When the bird opened his mouth to sing, his

entire throat and the inside of his bill glowed yellow. I had lived in Maine my whole life up until that point but I had never known that this bird—a Northern Parula—shared the woods with me each summer!

The Northern Parula proved to be my spark bird—the birding experience that launched me into the colorful, melodic, exciting world of bird-watching. From then on, I wanted to see birds wherever I explored. I later went back to school to study environmental science, then went on to work for the National Audubon Society—a conservation organization dedicated to protecting birds and the places they need the most.

What will your spark bird be?

Northern Parula

Barn Swallow

About Birds

Go outside. Stop, look, listen. Chances are, you will notice a bird. From dense cities to open oceans, dry deserts to tall mountains, birds have adapted to live in habitats around the world.

What is a bird? Birds are vertebrates (they have bones), but they also have feathers. This makes them unlike all other creatures on Earth. Today, there are more than 10,000 distinct species of birds spread out across the far corners of the globe.

Birds share five major traits:

1) They have feathers. Birds are the only animals on the planet with feathers.

Great Egret

Atlantic Puffin

2) Though not all birds fly, they all have wings. There are five general types of wings: one allows better soaring using thermals, one is better suited for soaring on wind currents, one is used for making quick turns in the air, one is used for flying quickly for a long time, and one is best for hovering.

3) They all have beaks, though the beaks vary in size, shape, and color. Beaks are used for eating, cleaning feathers, building nests, and so much more.

4) They have lightweight, hollow bones. Because the bones are hollow, birds can actually use them to help breathe when tiny air sacs in the lungs move into the space in the bones.

5) They lay eggs. The largest eggs are laid by Ostriches, and the smallest come from the Bee Hummingbird!

How Birds Evolved
THE BASICS OF EVOLUTION

How does evolution work? When babies are born, they may be very similar to all the other babies born to that species, but they also have key differences. Some of these differences will help them survive and have their own babies, who then inherit that special trait. For example, on the Galapagos Islands, certain finches were born with bigger bills that could crush seeds more easily. Over time, the finches with bigger bills had more babies, who in turn had bigger bills, until these finches looked very different from their original ancestor.

The birds we know today are direct descendants of the dinosaurs.

Around 66 million years ago, something happened—we are still not sure what, but it may have been a collision with an asteroid—that caused 80% of the species on Earth to go extinct. Nearly all dinosaurs disappeared, but some survived!

When other dinosaurs died out, scientists theorize that some theropod dinosaurs—which had two legs—survived by eating seeds. These dinosaurs were already small, grew feathers, and sported sharp teeth.

Pileated Woodpecker

Archaeopteryx, a bird relative

Over millions of years, their teeth disappeared and they developed bills. They became even smaller and lighter, evolving into the sizes and shapes of the birds we know today, which in turn made flight easier.

Reptiles

Mammals   Turtles   Lizards &   Crocodiles   Birds
                     Snakes

This cladogram classifies mammals, reptiles, and birds in clades based on their evolutionary relationships. On the cladogram, birds are closer to crocodiles, so they are more closely related than birds are to mammals, for instance.

Flight & Anatomy
HOW DO BIRDS FLY?

Birds have very lightweight bones and strong breast muscles. When they pump their wings—which are long and flat—the pressure from air flowing under their wing feathers is stronger than the pressure pushing down on them from above, and they can fly! But wait, why is there less pressure above? That all comes down to wing shape. The curve of the upper part of

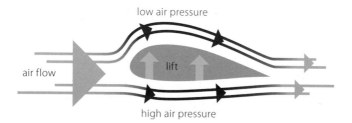

low air pressure

air flow   lift

high air pressure

a bird's wing means air has to move across a longer space to get across the wing, making it move faster.

ANATOMY

It's important to know your bird anatomy because that will help you learn field marks—ways to identify a bird in the outdoors. Birds can have different colored feathers across their bodies: if you know the parts, you know what to look for!

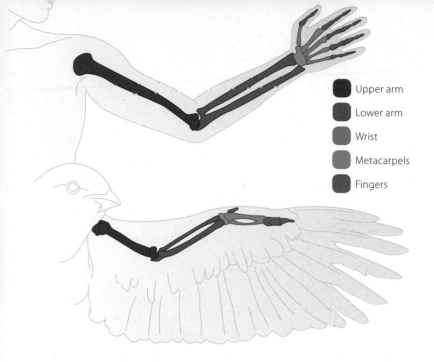

Upper arm
Lower arm
Wrist
Metacarpels
Fingers

FEATHERS

There are a lot of different types of feathers in the bird world! Each feather, however, is made up of the strong, middle part—known as the rachis—and the connecting barbs, which are like branches on a tree. The barbules are the smallest parts on a feather and the most numerous. The arrangement and structure of these three parts lead to different feather types. Some are warm and downy to keep chicks protected, while others are long and stiff to help birds soar.

There are seven general types of feathers: wing (for flight), down (to keep warm), tail (for steering), contour (for covering a bird's body and keeping water out), semiplume (for insulation), bristle (to protect birds' faces), and filoplume (they act like whiskers).

Rachis

Vane

Barb

Rachis

Barbule

Afterfeather

Downy barbs

Hooklets

Barb

Hollow shaft, calamus

Barbule

Life Cycle

EGGS Birds lay eggs, then keep them warm so the chicks can develop inside the eggs. Sometimes both parents keep the eggs warm, sometimes just the mom, sometimes just the dad.

European Starling

CHICKS Once chicks hatch, many need to be fed by their parents until they grow strong enough to feed on their own (these are known as altricial chicks). There are exceptions: precocial chicks, like plovers, can feed by themselves, but they need the protection of their parents against predators. Most chicks are born with soft, downy feathers that can make them look like little fuzzballs, but they eventually grow adult feathers.

JUVENILES Juvenile birds are not quite adults yet. They may look different than adults because they don't have all their adult feathers, or they don't have the plumage colors of adults. They are usually adult-size, but they may still need help learning how to feed and protect themselves.

In some species, juveniles—known as fledglings— have left the nest but aren't quite able to fly. You may find these birds on the ground, but don't worry, they aren't hurt. Their parents are probably close by, still protecting and feeding the fledglings. While you can watch and enjoy their antics, don't disturb them or approach them too closely.

ADULTS Adult birds are mature enough to breed, make nests, and have chicks of their own!

egg

nesting

adult

juvenile

chicks

NEST TYPES Birds have eight different nest types—some are used for years, while others are meant to only last a few days. Some birds have no nests at all; they use nests built by other species.

Large, longer-lasting nests: These nests are often built from large branches or twigs, and lined with softer materials like sod or seaweed. Ducks and some seabirds (like loons) also make larger nests on the ground, though they don't typically last beyond one season.

Small, stretchy nests: instead of twigs, these nests are built from plant fibers, hair, or even spider webs.

Bag nests: these structures are typically sewn or woven using a variety of materials, including grass and animal hair.

Scoop nests: Shorebirds and seabirds that nest on beaches hardly have any nests at all. They make depressions in the sand and incubate their eggs right there! The advantage of this? The eggs are well-camouflaged.

Cliff/rock/island nests: Seabirds that nest on cliffs use the natural depressions or crevices in the rock to lay their eggs.

Grass nests: Some duck species build their nests near the water or on floating grasses. To keep the eggs from sinking, they use reeds and other

plants to create a nest, then tie or anchor their floating home to water plants growing nearby.

Nest cavities: These species, which range from owls to ducks to woodpeckers, nest in cavities. Cavities include, but are not limited to: cactus holes, tree holes, caves, nest boxes, and more.

EGGS

Eggs come in a huge variety of shapes and sizes. The largest eggs in the world—laid by the Ostrich—are 6 inches long, while the smallest—which come from Bee Hummingbirds—only weigh half a gram!

How do eggs get their color?

Eggs can be as blue as the sky, as white as bone, or speckled—just like freckles! But all egg colors come from the combination of only two pigments:

1) Protoporphyrin makes eggs either red or brown.

2) Biliverdin makes eggs either green or blue. Like in your paint set, if you mix them together in different amounts, you get a different egg color.

Some eggs are speckled to help them blend in with their background environment. Because eggs have no defenses against predators, camouflage helps protect them if the parents are away. By contrast, eggs that can't easily be seen—like those in nest cavities—tend to be white.

What are eggs made of?

All eggshells are made from calcium carbonate. Though the shell is hard, water and air can still pass through, making it a semipermeable (breathable) membrane. The hard cuticle layer, on the very outside of the shell, keeps dust and bacteria from getting in.

Anatomy of a Bird Embryo

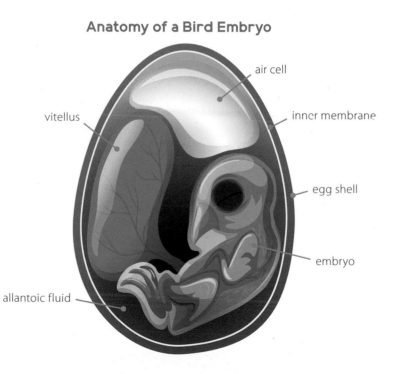

air cell

vitellus

inner membrane

egg shell

embryo

allantoic fluid

Turkey Vulture soaring on thermals

Different Kinds of Flight

Did you know that birds use different flight patterns?
Species have adapted to their environments and what
they eat (or what eats them), and have developed
their flight to survive.

SOARING (THERMALS)

Many raptors and seabirds use soaring to fly long
distances. These species typically have wings that lock
in place to reduce the energy needed for flying. Some
species can even fall asleep while flying! They use
updrafts—also called thermals—of moving air currents to stay aloft, rather than beating their wings.

HOVERING (HUMMINGBIRDS)

By flapping their wings vigorously—which uses up a lot of energy—birds can hover in place like a helicopter. Though hummingbirds are most known for this behavior, it is occasionally seen in larger birds, too, like Osprey, kites, or Belted Kingfishers.

DIVING (FALCONS/SOME SEABIRDS)

To catch food, birds can dive quickly through the air, surprising prey on the ground, in the air, or in the water. Peregrine Falcons can reach speeds up to 240 miles an hour as they zip through the sky. Osprey also dive for prey on the surface of the water, starting the plunge as high as 120 feet into the air.

DARTING

When birds depend on patchier habitat or food, they are known to dart from place to place, tree to tree, or from cover to cover.

FLIGHTLESS BIRDS OR BIRDS THAT DON'T FLY EASILY

Some birds have made evolutionary trade-offs: they need heavier bones to fish beneath the surface of the water, but it makes it more difficult to fly. Loons need to be able to sink to the bottom to look for food, but because they are so much heavier, they need large distances in order to successfully take off. To move fast enough to lift off, they sometimes need to run along the surface of the water for a quarter of a mile!

And, of course, some birds cannot fly at all. Penguins use their wings to swim underwater. Though they can no longer take off, they are well adapted to chasing

fish and other prey beneath the waves.

Migration

More than 350 bird species in North America migrate short or long distances. Though each species has a different migratory path, they all move north for the summer breeding season, then south again to return to their wintering grounds. Birds are on the move during both spring and summer—known as migration seasons.

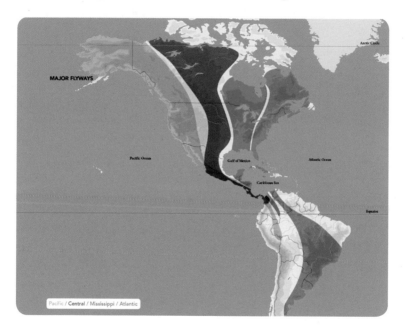

Why do birds migrate?

Migration has its costs. Birds that fly over open water can be caught in storms or lose energy, eventually falling into the sea or ocean. Migrating birds are vulnerable to predators, as well as human disruption in the forms of power lines and buildings. But the risk is worth it because the birds need the higher level of resources found in the northern breeding grounds in order to successfully raise their chicks.

If a bird nests in the northern half of the world, they tend to move north during the spring months to nest in northern areas where there is an explosion of insects, new plants, and also a lot of open nesting territory. Why do they leave again in the fall? It gets cold! As winter sets in, food declines, so the birds head south for warmer conditions and more to eat.

IRRUPTION YEARS

Sometimes, birds that usually migrate short distances—or even species that don't migrate at all—move far beyond their normal range. While there are multiple factors at work, irruptions are generally driven by food shortages. For example, Snowy Owls move farther south than normal when not enough food can be found in their usual northern hunting grounds. These years can directly follow boom years, when more owls

are born and make it into adulthood. When high population levels combine with a subsequent year of lower food sources, the owls need to move to survive.

What does this mean for you as a birder?

During different times of the year, you have the opportunity to see different bird species! Spring and summer are especially popular birding times, because in addition to

spotting the birds that may breed or winter where you live, you may have able to see dozens if not hundreds more birds as they pass through on their way north or south.

Which bird has the longest migration path?

The Arctic Tern! Arctic Terns migrate every year from the Arctic to the Antarctic and back again—

that's 90,000 km every single year. Because they live to be about 30 years old, that means these remarkable terns travel enough in their lifetime to equal the distance between the Earth and the moon six times over.

Western Tanager   American Goldfinch   American Goldfinch winter

Changing Plumage

Plumage—also known as a bird's feathers—communicates important information about birds. Depending on the color of a bird's feathers, we can tell if we are looking at a chick, juvenile, or adult, and in some cases whether the bird is male or female. Many migratory species have duller colors in the winter months, after which the males brighten up considerably to attract a mate during breeding season. In general, males are much more colorful than the females, who keep their duller plumage year-round in order to better hide from predators. Don't the males need to hide from predators? Yes, but it is more important for them to demonstrate their health and vitality to the females, who will then choose them for a mate. In the eyes of the females, the brighter the feathers, the healthier the bird.

Bird Types
SONGBIRDS

female Northern Parula

Does a songbird always have a beautiful voice? Not necessarily.

If you are a scientist, when you say "songbird" you mean a specific group of birds. Songbirds are all passerines—which means they are perching birds. Passerines, in turn, are divided into three smaller groups—one of which we call songbirds! More than 4,000 species are considered songbirds, from large Common Ravens to small Northern Parulas.

Another trait that sets them apart: they are able to exert special control over their voice box, called a syrinx. American Robins, chickadees, Blue Jays, and wrens are just a few examples of songbirds.

RAPTORS

Also known as birds of prey, this species group eats meat they catch or scavenge. Raptors grasp prey or carrion with sharp talons and have specialized, sharp beaks for ripping and tearing. Hawks, vultures, owls, and eagles are all raptors.

SHOREBIRDS

Also known as waders, shore-birds are small species that use wetlands, beaches, coastlines, and intertidal areas to find food, often probing the mud or sand with their bills. Sanderlings, curlews, and stilts are just a few examples of shorebirds.

SEABIRDS

Seabirds may look very differ-ent, but they share one critical characteristic: they need oceans and seas to survive. Puffins, gulls, Black Skimmers, and loons are all seabirds.

WADING BIRDS

These birds are generally large with long legs, perfect for wading around in water or mud in search of prey. Ibises, herons, egrets, storks, and the American Flamingo (pg. 92) are all wading birds.

WATERFOWL

With both webbed feet and waterproof feathers, these birds are well-adapted to life on the water. Ducks, geese, and swans are all waterfowl.

PARROTS

There may be more than 400 species of parrots throughout the world, but there are very few that make their homes in North America. They are known for their curved bills and feet that have two toes that point forwards and two toes that point backwards. The Thick-billed Parrot is the only native breeding parrot still found in North America, but birders can still see independent populations of escaped birds, like Monk Parakeets.

HUMMINGBIRDS

Hummers, as they are sometimes known, are small and stubby, with super sharp, needle-like bills and a fast wingbeat that allows them to hover in place.

WOODPECKERS

Woodpeckers use their specially formed bills and skulls to pound into the trunks and branches of trees to find food and build nests. Because they do not have songs, they use their drumming to communicate. Northern Flickers, sapsuckers, and Pileated Woodpeckers are all examples of woodpecker species.

GAME BIRDS

Both native and introduced for hunting, game birds spend most of their time in upland habitats. Turkey, grouse, and partridges are all game birds.

Habitat

SALTWATER

Saltwater habitats include the open ocean as well as coastal areas. Birds utilize bays, sounds, marshes, and beaches to feed and raise their young. In these areas, keep a sharp eye out for wading birds, shorebirds, and seabirds.

FRESHWATER

Freshwater habitats include rivers, lakes, swamps, and ponds. Birds use these areas to find food as well as raise their young. Look for waterfowl, Osprey, Belted Kingfishers, and wading birds.

NEIGHBORHOODS (SUBURBS)

Many bird species have adapted to live near humans. Look for birds in trees, in yard bushes or plants, or flying

overhead. Plant native plants to bring more birds to your yard. In these areas, look for songbirds, wood-peckers, doves, and Northern Mockingbirds.

CITIES

Yes, birds can live in cities too! Hawk species utilize buildings (which to them seem like giant cliffs), nesting in the crevices. Also look for pigeons, Common Grackles, House Sparrows (an invasive species), and European Starlings (another invasive species). City parks often attract many songbirds during the migration season.

GRASSLANDS

Open grasslands are characterized by a lack of trees and bushes as well as the dominance of grasses as the main type of vegetation. Grasslands

host many unique bird species. In these areas, also look for cranes, songbirds, game birds (including grouse), and raptors.

MOUNTAINS

Many species are specially adapted to higher altitudes, and can be found nowhere else. They may be related to bird species found at lower elevations, but have evolved for the more extreme alpine conditions. Look for specific species of songbirds, including wrens, chickadees, and thrush.

FORESTS

The United States is home to many kinds of forests, from the mangroves of Florida to the pine woods of Maine to the rainforests of the Pacific Northwest and so much more. The type of forest influences which birds call these areas home. Look for songbirds, woodpeckers, and owls.

WETLANDS

Wetlands are, quite simply, areas where water covers the soil. Swamps, seasonal ponds, peatlands, marshes, and bogs are all examples of wetlands. Note: Wetlands can be part of both freshwater and saltwater ecosystems as well.

Birds found in these areas are highly dependent on the location, but wetlands generally attract shore-birds (especially during migration), wading birds, and songbirds attracted to the open air above the water.

DESERTS

Deserts are characterized by their lack of water, and can often be quite hot or very cold. In general, scientists agree that areas that receive less than 10 inches of rain per year become deserts. Birds here are well adapted to the harsh conditions—look for raptors, roadrunners, quail, wrens, and woodpeckers.

Cactus Wren

Conservation

In the 1800s, thousands and thousands and thousands of Passenger Pigeons could darken the sky with their sheer numbers as they moved from one area to another. Scientists think that at one time they could have been the most populous birds in the world, with millions of breeding birds.

Passenger Pigeon

In the mid-19th century, Simon Pokagon, a Potawami leader, heard a loud, rumbling sound while camping. "As I listened more intently," he said later, as he described the experience, "I concluded that instead of the trumping of horses it was distant thunder; and yet the morning was clear, calm, and beautiful. Nearer and nearer came the strange comingling sound of sleigh bells, mixed with the rumbling storm." Finally, he figured out the source of the noise: "While I gazed in wonder and astonishment, I beheld moving toward me in an unbroken front millions of pigeons, the first I had seen that season."

Unfortunately, hunting and decimation of their nesting grounds starting to shrink their population, and by the end of the 19th century their numbers had collapsed. In 1914, the very last Passenger Pigeon died at the Cincinnati Zoo. The species had gone extinct.

Hunting combined with habitat loss drove multiple North American bird species to extinction, including Carolina Parakeets, Ivory-billed Woodpeckers, Eskimo Curlews, and the Great Auk. Back then, little to no hunting regulations existed to protect these species, and as the populations of European-descendent settlers increased, the number of birds declined. Hunters shot birds for food, but also for fashion, as ladies' hats prized colorful feathers for decoration. The introduction of invasive species—including cats and dogs—continues to harm bird populations. Cats alone kill more than 2 billion birds every year. The effect is especially damaging on islands, where birds have often evolved without predators.

As the 1800s drew to a close, people began to sound the alarm: Without action, more birds would soon be extinct.

Passenger Pigeon

Carolina Parakeet

Ivory-billed Woodpecker

Eskimo Curlew

Great Auk

STOPPING THE PLUME TRADE

Few feathers were more prized for hats than the beautiful breeding feathers—also known as aigrettes—grown by wading birds. Plume hunters could destroy large colonies in just a few days, sending thousands and thousands of feathers to hat-making centers like New York and London in a single year. In 1915, hunters could sell plume feathers for more than $30 per ounce—the same price as gold.

For the species that faced hunting for their feathers, extinction became a real threat.

An advertisement

In 1896, Harriet Lawrence Hemenway of Boston read an article about the horrors of the plume trade and determined to act. She joined forces with her cousin Minna Hall to start speaking with their friends about the damage their decorated hats caused bird populations across the United States, demanding a stop. According to the *Smithsonian Magazine*, Hall remembered: "We sent out circulars, asking the women to join a society for the protection of birds, especially the egret. Some women joined and some who preferred to wear feathers would not join."

Persuaded that they needed to change fashion in order to save the beautiful bird species, hundreds of

Great Egret and aigrettes

women declared that they would no longer wear hats with feathers. Their actions and commitment led to the formation of the Massachusetts Audubon Society to continue their work to protect vulnerable bird species. When other Audubon Societies were formed, the group leaders decided to band together to create a unified, stronger organization. In 1905, they merged to become the National Audubon Society, which still protects birds and their habitats today.

Congress passed the Lacey Act in 1900, the very first law that the U.S. government could use to protect wildlife. Under this new rule, you could not take feathers from one state to another, which meant hunters couldn't take the feathers from wading birds in the Southeast to hat-making areas in the Northeast. Still, it was a difficult law to enforce, and

MUST GIVE UP AIGRETTES

Audubon Society Issues Urgent Appeal to Women.

The Audubon societies, thru their organ, Bird-Lore, make an urgent appeal to the women of America to abstain from using aigrettes. It is claimed that the herons from which these aigrette plumes are taken are rapidly approaching extinction. The dealers' offer of $32 per ounce for raw plumes tempts hunters to defy the law, and it is believed that if woman does not abandon the use of aigrettes the white herons thruout the world will be exterminated.

Bird-Lore publishes a detailed statement of the facts in the case by William Dutcher, which can be obtained in leaflet from the national committee of Audubon societies, 525 Manhattan avenue, New York city.

Convention of Rebekahs.

the hunters could be violent. In 1905, a plume hunter killed Guy Bradley, a warden in Florida tasked with protecting the birds. This led to a national outcry, and those who wanted to save the birds put more pressure on the government to act.

In 1913, the Weeks-McLean Law passed to stop the plume trade once and for all. It read:

"All wild geese, wild swans, brant, wild ducks, snipe, plover, woodcock, rail, wild pigeons, and all other migratory game and insectivorous birds which in their northern and southern migrations pass through or do not remain permanently the entire year within the borders of any State or Territory, shall hereafter be deemed to be within the custody and protection of the Government of the United States, and shall not be destroyed or taken contrary to regulations hereinafter provided therefore."

Snowy Egret

What does that mean? That migratory birds cannot be killed.

This law was eventually replaced by the Migratory Bird Treaty Act of 1918, which has protected birds in the United States for more than 100 years.

BANNING DDT

While many birds were now safe from hunting, other environmental problems still threatened species with extinction. In the 1900s, people across the country sprayed a pesticide known as DDT to kill mosquitoes and other insects that caused human diseases like malaria and typhus.

DDT also decimated the bird populations. Rachel Carson, a biologist and writer, investigated the connections between widespread pesticide use and declining bird populations, publishing *Silent Spring* in 1962 to warn people that more birds could disappear if Americans didn't stop the use of certain pesticides, including DDT.

When DDT was sprayed, it accumulated in both the soil and in the food web. Wildlife that ate plants also absorbed DDT, and when they were eaten by the next animal up the food chain, that species accumulated an

even larger amount of the toxin in their bodies. By the time the pesticide reached the top animal in the food chain—carnivorous birds like Bald Eagles and Osprey—the raptors had so much of the pesticide in their bodies that they could no longer can live normally.

For birds of prey, the DDT made their eggshells too thin and too breakable. Parent birds couldn't successfully raise chicks, and their populations plummeted.

Peregrine Falcon

After Carson published *Silent Spring*, a new generation of environmentalists and bird lovers worked to ban DDT and other dangerous pesticides. President Nixon established the Environmental Protection Agency in 1970 to better regulate these chemicals, and in 1972 DDT was banned.

Since then, populations of many raptors have recovered, aided by protections afforded by the Endangered Species Act (ESA), passed in 1973. The ESA built upon the Endangered Species Preservation Act of 1966, which instructed government agencies to list species in danger of going extinct and provide some protections. ESA went further, and hurting or killing threatened or endangered species became illegal, with more funding available to bring these vulnerable plants and animals back from the brink. The Endangered Species Act has been instrumental in the recovery of Bald Eagles, Brown Pelicans, Grizzly Bears, Humpback Whales, and more.

Are there things we still need to do to help the birds? Absolutely!

Researchers estimate that we have lost nearly 3 billion birds since 1970, and the National Audubon Society warns that 389 species could go extinct if we do not curb climate change.

Brown Pelican in flight

CLIMATE CHANGE

Climate change is the biggest threat to birds—and people—in the twenty-first century.

In the Industrial Revolution, fossil fuels such as coal became important energy sources. Later, other fossil fuels such as oil and natural gas became important sources of electricity, not to mention fuel for cars. But when we burn fossil fuels, carbon dioxide is released into the atmosphere. Once in the sky, the carbon dioxide traps heat that would otherwise escape. Over time the higher concentration of carbon dioxide in the atmosphere has heated the planet, and it will continue to do so as long as we burn additional fossil fuels.

Scientists estimate that global temperatures will continue to increase, which in turn will affect the weather across the globe. Sea levels are expected to rise as ice caps melt, and heat from our warmer oceans and seas will create stronger and more frequent storms. In some places, more rain will fall, but in others, the climate will become increasingly dry.

All these changes are happening in a very short period of time, and birds cannot adapt quickly enough. Sea level rise and storms threaten to swamp coastal nesting species, while drier conditions means less food for hungry birds and their chicks. While some birds will move to survive, others do not have that option. For example, some birds are specifically adapted to cooler, mountain environments. As the climate warms, these ecosystems have nowhere to move, as the mountains cannot become any taller!

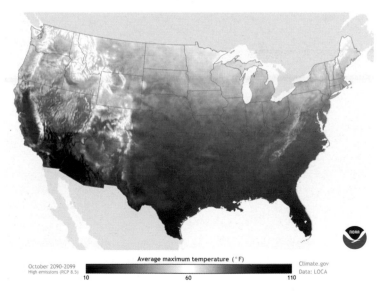

Average maximum temperature (°F)

October 2090-2099
High emissions (RCP 8.5)

10   60   110

Climate.gov
Data: LOCA

This NOAA projection shows average temperatures in October 2090 if carbon dioxide emissions remain high

Getting Started as a Birder

The only thing you really need to be a good birder is curiosity about the natural world. You can see birds everywhere, from the pigeons and sparrows of the city to the robins and jays of suburban neighborhoods to the meadowlarks and bluebirds of open fields.

Look at each bird carefully, and if it helps, take notes on what you observe. What color are they, and where are the colors on the bird's body? What does the bill look like? Approximately how big is the bird? Importantly, note the habitat in which the bird appears. Some species, like Belted Kingfishers, are only found near water, while others, including Pine Warblers, prefer specific species of trees. The more you bird, the more these relationships will stand out to you.

Though you don't need anything but your eyes and ears for birding, there are a few tools to help make identification easier.

Binoculars

Binoculars zoom in on the bird, making it easier to spot a bird's distinguishing field marks, or traits, that distinguish it from other species.

Camera If you have a camera with a zoom lens, you can take a photo of the bird you see and use field guides or the internet to help make an identification.

Field guides Field guides are illustrated with drawings or photographs to show you how to tell different bird species apart. Today, there are online field guides and apps, like the Merlin ID app by the Cornell Lab of Ornithology or the Bird Guide App by the National Audubon Society.

Notebook A notebook is super helpful to keep track of the birds you see, the field marks you notice, as well as your observations about bird habitat.

Where and How to Look
BASIC RULES OF BIRDING:

Do not wear white or bright colors—opt for greens or browns to blend into the environment.

Shhh! Birds can be spooked by loud noises—stay quiet when possible.

Leave pets at home—they scare birds and make noise.

HOW TO CHOOSE A BIRDING LOCATION

Pick a spot with lots of different habitats because that will attract a variety of bird species. Coastal locations with marsh or upland habitats, or forests with lakes or rivers are examples of multiple habitat types together in one place.

Are you looking for specific types of birds, like desert species or beach birds? Go to those habitat types! Knowing what kinds of places birds like is the best way to find them.

Are you looking for a specific species? Know both their habitats and habits. For example, Bald Eagles soar through the air or perch in a tree—especially near water—but won't generally be found on the ground, like a turkey, or eating roadkill like a Black Vulture. Common Loons in the summer need bigger bodies of water in order to successfully take off, so you won't find them on small ponds or narrow rivers.

HOW TO IDENTIFY BIRDS

To identify birds, use binoculars, a camera, or your eyes to take in their field marks, jotting them down for identification in a field guide or using photographs on the internet (with a parent's permission).

What if you can't see the birds? You can identify them by their calls! This is especially important for shy birds that are easily spooked. Rails—chicken-like species that live between the reeds in the marshes—are almost impossible to see. Luckily, they make a lot of clapping and keking noises that birders can use to identify them. Similarly, owls are active at night when they are difficult to see, but their calls echo through the sky and are easily identifiable.

To identify bird calls, listen to them ahead of time using internet recordings so you can recognize the sounds when out in nature. The free Merlin Bird ID app can also help—just hold up your phone towards the call!

KEEPING BIRDS SAFE

Whenever and wherever you bird, make sure you are considerate of the species you see. Don't approach too closely because that could scare the birds. Stay away from nests. If you play songs to attract birds closer to you, do so sparingly, as this interrupts their usual activities and causes the birds to expend a lot of energy. On beaches, do not walk through flocks of birds—they need their rest, and they may be near nesting locations.

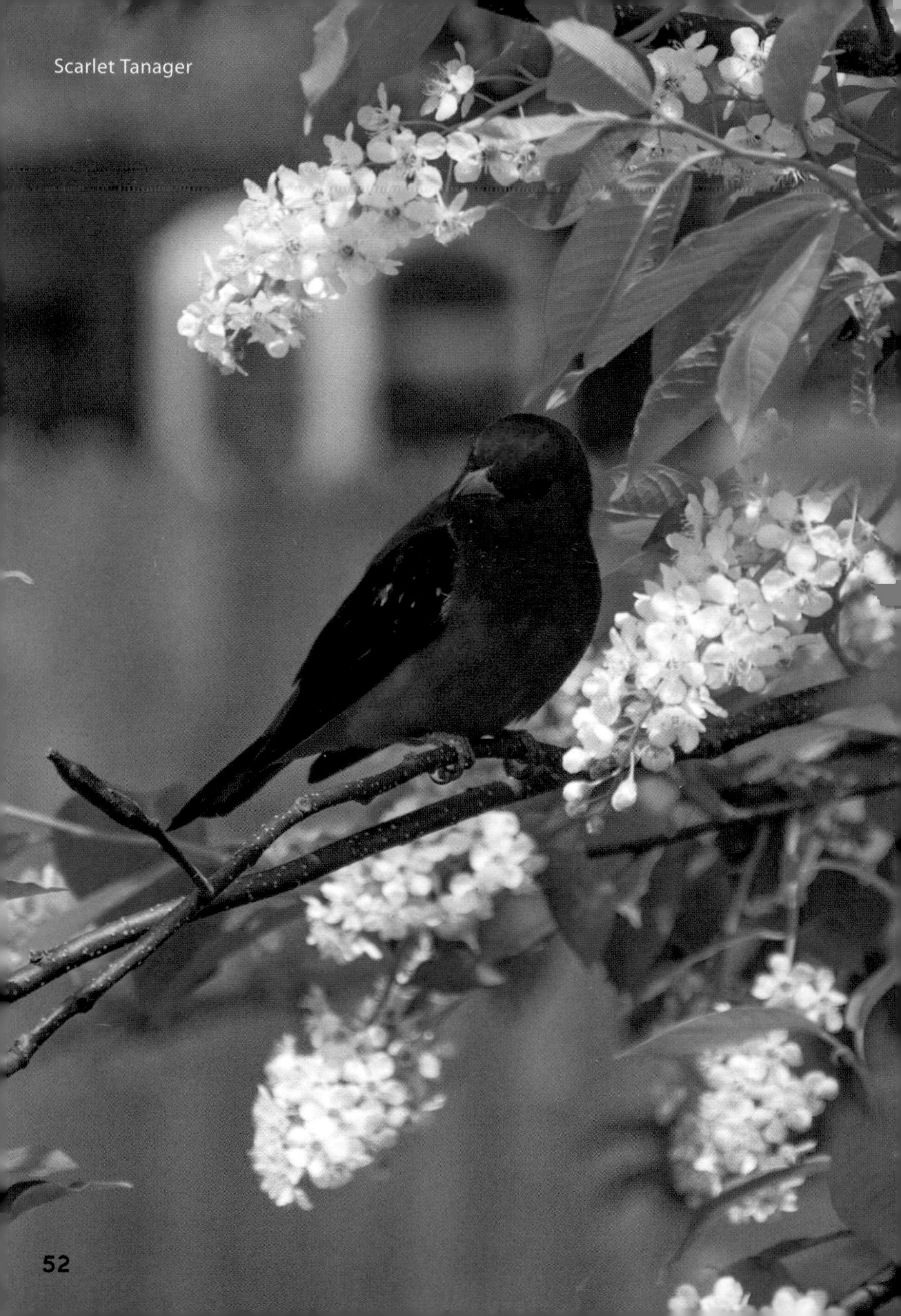
Scarlet Tanager

The Birds

The best way to begin learning your bird species is by first recognizing your backyard birds. Usually song-birds and woodpeckers, these species are known to come to bird feeders and berry bushes, which means you will have a lot of time to get to know them!

Eastern

Western

EASTERN AND WESTERN BLUEBIRD

When you'll see them: Year-round.

Where you'll see them: Eastern Bluebirds can be seen in the northern states in the Eastern half of the country in the summer months, and in the southern half year-round. Western Bluebirds are found year-round in parts of California and the Southwest, while they move to the Pacific Northwest and parts of Colorado in the breeding season.

Look for: Blue heads and backs with orange chests.

Comes to feeders: Yes, to mealworms. They may also nest in nest boxes if you live in a semi-wooded area.

BROWN THRASHER

When you'll see them: Year-round in the Southeast, during the summer months in the northern half of the eastern United States.

Where you'll see them: Eastern half of the United States.

Look for: Reddish-brown head and back, heavily streaked chest and stomach.

Comes to feeders: They will come to yards with berry-bearing shrubs, and will sometimes eat seed that has fallen beneath a feeder.

CEDAR WAXWING

When you'll see them: Year-round in the northern half of the United States; summer only in the southern half of the United States.

Where you'll see them: Across the United States.

Look for: Large brownish crest with black face mask, darker wings and yellow belly fading to white by the tail. The ends of their tails look like they've been dipped in yellow ink.

Comes to feeders: Yes, to fruit on a platform feeder. They also love bushes and trees that bear fruit.

PAINTED BUNTING

When and where you'll see them: In Texas, Louisiana, Oklahoma, Arkansas, parts of Mississippi, Kansas, and Missouri, as well as along the Southeastern coast in the summer. They migrate across the Southeast in the spring and fall, and can be found in the winter in South Florida.

Look for: Brilliantly colored, males have bright-red stomachs, blue heads, and green and red backs; females are a more uniform green.

Comes to feeders: Yes. They prefer seeds in a bird feeder with plenty of nearby cover.

LAZULI BUNTING

When you'll see them: Summer and during migration.

Where you'll see them: Western half of the United States.

Look for: Sky-blue head, back, and wings, with orange chest above a white stomach.

Comes to feeders: Yes. They will eat millet, thistle seeds, and sunflower seeds.

DARK EYED JUNCO

When you'll see them: Summer in Alaska, year-round in the Northeast and western half of the United States; winter in the southern half of the United States other than the northeastern states.

Where you'll see them: Across the United States, depending on the season.

Look for: There are multiple color morphs of the Dark-eyed Junco, depending on your region, but in general they are dark birds with pale stomachs and pink bills.

Comes to feeders: Yes. They will eat sunflower seeds, oats, millet, milo, nyjer, safflower, and peanuts.

VARIED THRUSH

When and where you'll see them: California in the winter months; along the coast of Washington and Oregon year-round, and farther inland during the winter; into Alaska, Idaho, and Montana in the summer.

Look for: Gray-backed bird about the size of a robin, with a bright-orange throat and chest with a gray chest band.

Comes to feeders: Yes. They like to come to yards with shrubs that bear fruit, but will also come to feeders that scatter seed on the ground.

AMERICAN ROBIN

When you'll see them: Year-round.

Where you'll see them: Across the United States.

Look for: Dark head and back but bright-orange chest and stomach.

Comes to feeders: Yes. They aren't picky, and will eat mealworms, suet, fruit, peanuts, and sunflower seeds.

AMERICAN GOLDFINCH

When you'll see them: Year-round in most of the United States; during winter in the Southeast, Southwest, as well as California, and in the summer in the most northern states.

Where you'll see them: Across the United States.

Look for: A bright-yellow bird with black wings and a black forehead.

Comes to feeders: Yes. They will use most feeders and prefer sunflower seeds and nyjer, but will also come to your yard if you plant thistles and milkweed.

SONG SPARROW

When you'll see them: Winter in the southern states, summer in North Dakota, year-round everywhere else.

Where you'll see them: Across the United States.

Look for: The streaks on its chest come together to form a dense spot.

Comes to feeders: Yes.

BLUE JAY

When you'll see them: Year-round.

Where you'll see them: Most common in the eastern United States.

Look for: Bright-blue back, large crest, and white stomach.

Comes to feeders: Yes. They prefer platform bird feeders and love peanuts, corn, and sunflower seeds.

NORTHERN CARDINAL
When you'll see them:
Year-round.

Where you'll see them: Most common in the eastern United States, plus Texas and Arizona.

Look for: Males are bright red, while females are more brown—both have a large crest on their heads.

Comes to feeders: Yes. Black-oil sunflowers are their favorite.

NORTHERN MOCKINGBIRD
When you'll see them:
Year-round.

Where you'll see them: Across the United States.

Look for: A gray bird with a long tail, singing loudly and often.

Comes to feeders: Yes, for suet and cut fruit.

MOURNING DOVE

When you'll see them: Year-round in all but the most northern states in the Midwest; those areas have summer-only populations.

Where you'll see them: Across the country.

Look for: Brown dove with pinkish breast.

Comes to feeders: Yes, especially to millet spread on the ground.

GRAY CATBIRD

When and where you'll see them: Across the country in the summer months, except California, Nevada, and most of Arizona and Oregon. They are found year-round in parts of Texas, Louisiana, Florida, and the Atlantic coast states up to New England.

Look for: A slate-gray bird with a black cap. Comes to feeders: They prefer fruits, so plant fruiting shrubs in your yard.

CHICKADEES

There are seven species of chickadees within the United States. Use where you live to figure out which one you are seeing!

When you'll see them: Year-round.

Look for: A small songbird with a dark cap.

Comes to feeders: Yes. Chickadees love sunflower seeds and suet.

Black-capped Chickadee
Northern half of the United States

Carolina Chickadee
Southeastern United States

Gray-headed Chickadee
Very limited range in parts of Alaska

Mexican Chickadee
Limited range in parts of Arizona and New Mexico

Boreal Chickadee
Northern parts of states that border Canada

Chestnut-backed Chickadee
California, Pacific Northwest

Mountain Chickadee
Mountain areas in the West

Many backyard birds are woodpecker species! Wood-peckers use their specially formed bills and skulls to pound into the trunks and branches of trees to find food and build nests. Because they do not have songs, they use their drumming to communicate. Northern Flickers, sapsuckers, and Pileated Woodpeckers are all examples of woodpecker species.

RED-BELLIED WOODPECKER

When you'll see them: Year-round.

Where you'll see them: Eastern half of United States.

Look for: A medium-size woodpecker with a bright-red head, white face, and black-and-white back.

Comes to feeders: Yes, for suet and peanuts.

PILEATED WOODPECKER

When you'll see them: Year-round.

Where you'll see them: Eastern half of United States, the Pacific Northwest.

Look for: A large woodpecker with a large, bright-red crest.

Comes to feeders: Occasionally, if there is suet available.

Downy

Hairy

DOWNY AND HAIRY WOODPECKER

When you'll see them: Year-round.

Where you'll see them: Across the United States.

Look for: A very small black-and-white woodpecker—males have a red spot on the back of their heads.

Comes to feeders: Yes

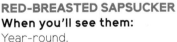

RED-BREASTED SAPSUCKER

When you'll see them: Year-round.

Where you'll see them: California, Oregon, and Washington.

Look for: Bright-red head and chest, with a dark back.

Comes to feeders: Yes.

Does a songbird have to have a beautiful voice?
Not necessarily.

Because there are more than 4,000 species of
songbirds, you are sure to see one on your birding
adventures! They vary widely in color, shape, and size,
but they may not have a beautiful singing voice.

Another trait that sets them apart: they are able to
exert special control over their voice box, called a
syrinx. American Robins, chickadees, Blue Jays, and
wrens are just a few examples of songbirds.

VERMILLION FLYCATCHER
When you'll see them: It
depends (see below).

Where you'll see them: Parts
of the Southwest United States
year-round, and the southeastern
United States along the Gulf
Coast in the winter months. In the
summer they can also be seen
farther inland in Texas, as well as
in Nevada, New Mexico, Arizona,
and California.

Look for: Bright-red head and
chest and stomach, with a dark
back eye stripe.

Comes to feeders: No.

SCISSOR-TAILED FLYCATCHER

When you'll see them: Summer.

Where you'll see them: Texas, Oklahoma, parts of Arkansas, Missouri, Louisiana, and Kansas.

Look for: Gray head, back, and chest, fading to pink underneath the very, very long tail. Dark wings.

Comes to feeders: No, but will sometimes stop at berry bushes.

Loggerhead

Northern

LOGGERHEAD AND NORTHERN SHRIKES

When you'll see them: Year-round, depending on your region.

**Where you'll see them:
Loggerhead Shrikes:** Southern half of the United States year-round, into the summer in the Midwest and Northwest.

Northern Shrikes: Northern half of the United States in the winter; Alaska during the summer.

Look for: Gray bird overall, with black wings; black face mask; and dark, hooked bill.

Comes to feeders: They only come to feeders to hunt the other birds using the feeders.

BLACK-BILLED MAGPIE
When you'll see them: Year-round.

Where you'll see them: Northwest quarter of the United States and into southern Alaska.

Look for: The size of a crow, they have black heads, backs, and chest, with a white stomach and long, black tail. Their wings are blue and white.

Comes to feeders: Yes. To feeders with a platform as well as suet. They will eat fruit, cracked corn, sunflower seeds, peanuts, millet, and milo.

BARN SWALLOW
When you'll see them: Summer.

Where you'll see them: Across the United States.

Look for: In the air they have a distinctive forked tail, with a blue head and orange/red lower face, as well as a pale chest and stomach.

Comes to feeders: No.

MOUNTAIN BLUEBIRD

When and where you'll see them: In the Northwest part of the United States and Alaska in the summer months; year-round in California, Oregon, and parts of the Southwest; in the winter farther south and east in the southwestern states as well as more coastal California.

Look for: Azure blue above, paler blue below.

Comes to feeders: They will nest in nest boxes if you live in an open area with some clumps of trees or bushes available.

YELLOW WARBLER

When you'll see them: During migration in the Southeast; during the summer breeding season in the rest of the United States, including Alaska.

Where you'll see them: Across the United States.

Look for: Males are bright yellow with subtle chestnut-colored streaks on their chests; females are less bright with a greenish-yellow back.

Comes to feeders: No.

COMMON YELLOWTHROAT
When you'll see them: Summer.

Where you'll see them: Across the United States in the summer; in the southeast and California they can be seen year-round.

Look for: Males are bright yellow with a black mask and greenish-yellow back; females have similar coloration but without the black mask.

Comes to feeders: No.

COMMON RAVEN
When you'll see them: Year-round.

Where you'll see them: The western United States, northern United States, parts of the Appalachian mountains and New England.

Look for: All-black bird larger than a crow.

Comes to feeders: Yes, to pet food or grains or seeds. You might not want them to, though—once they are in your yard, they may eat the eggs or chicks of other nearby nesters.

AMERICAN CROW

When you'll see them: Year-round in most of the country.

Where you'll see them: Across the United States.

Look for: All-black bird larger than a robin.

Comes to feeders: No, but they will come in for peanuts.

Eastern

Western

EASTERN AND WESTERN MEADOWLARKS

When you'll see them: Year-round, except in northern states, when they are seen in the summer.

Where you'll see them: Eastern Meadowlarks are mostly found in the eastern half of the United States, while Western Meadow larks are found in the western half of the United States; they overlap in the Southwest.

Look for: Brown-backed bird with bright-yellow chest and throat, complete with a U-shaped black necklace.

Comes to feeders: Western Meadowlarks do not regularly come to bird feeders, but Eastern Meadowlarks might.

CLARK'S NUTCRACKER
When you'll see them:
Year-round.

Where you'll see them:
Mountain habitat in the western United States.

Look for: A large gray bird with black wings.

Comes to feeders: Sometimes, they will eat peanuts and suet.

NORTHERN PARULA
When you'll see them: Spring and summer.

Where you'll see them: The eastern United States.

Look for: A brightly colored bird with a blue back, yellow-and-orange chest and throat.

Comes to feeders: No.

SCARLET TANAGER

When you'll see them: Spring and summer.

Where you'll see them: The eastern United States.

Look for: Bright-red bird with black wings.

Comes to feeders: No, but they love berry plants.

YELLOW-HEADED BLACKBIRD

When and where you'll see them: Eastern half of the United States in the summer months, though they are only found in Texas, Oklahoma, Arkansas, Louisiana, and Missouri during migration seasons or the winter months.

Look for: A bright-yellow head and chest with a black body for the males; females have a brown/yellow head with a yellow throat and chest.

Comes to feeders: Yes, for seeds and other grain-based food.

Also known as birds of prey, this species group eats meat they catch or scavenge. Raptors grasp prey or carrion with sharp talons and have specialized, sharp beaks for ripping and tearing. Hawks, vultures, owls, and eagles are all raptors.

BARRED OWL
When you'll see them: Year-round.

Where you'll see them: The eastern United States, the northwestern United States.

Look for: Large, streaked owl with dark-black eyes.

Comes to feeders: No. Listen for their call, which sounds like "Who cooks for you?"

GREAT HORNED OWL
When you'll see them: Year-round.

Where you'll see them: Across the United States.

Look for: Large owls with ear-like tufts; bright-yellow eyes.

Comes to feeders: No. Listen for their call, which sounds like "hoo-hoo-hoo-hoo."

TURKEY VULTURE

When you'll see them: Year-round in the Southeast, Southwest, and coastal California; year-round in the rest of the Lower 48.

Where you'll see them: Across the United States.

Look for: Red, bald heads and silver wing edges.

Comes to feeders: No. Watch for them circling slowly in the sky.

BALD EAGLE

When you'll see them: Year-round in much of the United States, more prevalent in the winter months.

Where you'll see them: Across the United States.

Look for: Bright-while heads against dark-brown bodies. Juveniles are more mottled.

Comes to feeders: No.

juvenile

RED-TAILED HAWK
When you'll see them: Year-round.

Where you'll see them: Across the United States.

Look for: Their bright-red tails are visible even when flying, so look for the signature color and shape.

Comes to feeders: No.

OSPREY
When you'll see them: Year-round in the Southeast and parts of California and Oregon. During the winter months in California and Texas, during the summer in other coastal states and along the Great Lakes. Inland sightings possible on large bodies of water.

Where you'll see them: Near bodies of water (saltwater or freshwater).

Look for: Ospreys look black and white from far away, with bright-yellow eyes. They dive for fish on the surface of the water.

Comes to feeders: No. Look for Ospreys fishing in large bodies of fresh or saltwater.

SNOWY OWL

When you'll see them: Winter.

Where you'll see them: Northern states bordering Canada and New England.

Look for: White owls with black streaks; yellow eyes.

Comes to feeders: No. This owl, however, is often seen in the daytime, so keep your eyes peeled.

RED-SHOULDERED HAWK

When you'll see them: Year-round, except in New England, where they can be spotted during the summer months.

Where you'll see them: Eastern half of the United States.

Look for: Reddish chest, streaked with white, and black-and-white barred tail.

Comes to feeders: No.

These birds are generally large with long legs, perfect for wading around in water or mud in search of prey. Ibises, herons, egrets, storks, and the American Flamingo (pg. 92) are all wading birds.

GREAT EGRET
When you'll see them: Year-round.

Where you'll see them: Pacific Coast states, Atlantic Coast states, Gulf Coast states, less common in interior states but possible in the summer.

Look for: Bright white, very tall bird. Long yellow bill.

Comes to feeders: No. Look in ponds or lakes, along rivers, or on the coast.

GREAT BLUE HERON
When you'll see them: Year-round; more common in the summer in northern states.

Where you'll see them: Across the United States.

Look for: Large gray/blue bird. Very tall.

Comes to feeders: No. Look in ponds or lakes, along rivers, or on the coast.

ROSEATE SPOONBILL
When you'll see them: Year-round.

Where you'll see them: Florida, Gulf Coast states.

Look for: Large, bright-pink bird. Flat, spoon-like bill.

Comes to feeders: No. Look in ponds or lakes, along rivers, or on the coast.

GREEN HERON
When and where you'll see them: Across the eastern half of the United States and the Pacific Northwest in the summer months, along the Gulf Coast year-round, South Carolina, California, and parts of New Mexico year-round. They can also be spotted in parts of the Southwest during migration season.

Look for: A small heron with a green back, brown face, and yellow legs.

Comes to feeders: No.

Seabirds may look very different, but they share one critical characteristic: they need oceans and seas to survive. Puffins, gulls, Black Skimmers, and loons are all seabirds. With both webbed feet and waterproof feathers, these birds are well-adapted to life on the water. Waterfowl also depend on water. Ducks, geese, and swans are all waterfowl.

RING-BILLED GULL
When you'll see them: Year-round.

Where you'll see them: They winter along the Gulf, Atlantic, and Pacific Coasts; migrate through the central United States and New England; then spend the summer in the northern states.

Look for: The dark ring on their bright-yellow bills.

Comes to feeders: No.

HERRING GULL
When and where you'll see them: They winter along the Pacific Coast, the New England Coast, and across the Southeast before migrating through the United States and spending the summers in northern states and Alaska. They live year-round on the mid-Atlantic coast up to Maine.

Look for: Large gull with bright-red spot on its bill.

Comes to feeders: No.

LOONS

There are four species of loons commonly seen within the United States. Use where you live to figure out which one you are seeing!

Look for: A black-and-white checkered back, a white chest, and a long, heavy bill.

Comes to feeders: No

Red-throated Loon
Along the Pacific and Atlantic Coasts in the winter.

Yellow-billed Loon
Along the Pacific coast in the winter, in Alaska during the summer.

Common Loon
Along the Pacific and Atlantic Coasts in the winter, on northern lakes in the summer.

Pacific Loon
Along the Pacific coast in the winter, in Alaska during the summer.

CORMORANTS

When you'll see them: Year-round, but dependent on the species.

Look for: A large, nearly all-black seabird with bulky head and small, sharp hook at the end of its large bill.

Comes to feeders: No.

Red-faced Cormorant
Alaska

Neotropic Cormorant
Texas, sightings rare in the Southeast and Southwest.

Pelagic Cormorant
Pacific Coast all the way from California to Alaska.

Double-crested Cormorant
Across the United States, depending on the season.

Brandt's Cormorant
Pacific Coast up to Canada
year-round; winter only
in Alaska.

Great Cormorant
East Coast as far south as
South Carolina, but only in
the winter.

ATLANTIC PUFFIN
When you'll see them: During the summer months.

Where you'll see them: Maine.

Look for: Black-and-white bird about the size of a football, with a very large, bright-orange-and-black bill.

Comes to feeders: No.

SNOW GOOSE
When and where you'll see them: Migrates across the United States in large flocks during the spring and summer on the way to wintering grounds in Alaska and northern Canada. Winters in pockets across North America, including the mid-interior states, the Gulf Coast, the Mid-Atlantic, and parts of California and the Pacific Northwest.

Look for: Snow Geese come in two color morphs: the most common is the all-white goose with the pink bill, while blue morphs are blue-gray colored except for their white heads.

Comes to feeders: No.

CANADA GOOSE

When you'll see them: Year-round, though in the southern half of the US. they are more common in winter. In Alaska they are found in the summer months.

Where you'll see them: Across the United States.

Look for: Brown goose with black neck and head, white patch on face.

Comes to feeders: Sometimes, if they can scoop leftover grain from the ground. Canada Geese can be aggressive, so it is probably not a good idea to encourage them to come too close to your house. If you build a nesting platform in a pond or lake they may use it!

MALLARD

When you'll see them: Year-round; in winter in the Southeast and Southwest.

Where you'll see them: Across the United States.

Look for: Females are all brown, while males have a stunning emerald-green head.

Comes to feeders: No. They do occasionally swim in people's pools.

Also known as waders, shorebirds are small species that use wetlands, beaches, coastlines, and intertidal areas to find food, often probing the mud or sand with their bills. Sanderlings, curlews, and stilts are just a few examples of shorebirds.

WILLET

When and where you'll see them: Year-round along the Gulf Coast and Atlantic Ocean coast all the way up through the Mid-Atlantic; in summer on the Atlantic Coast up through Maine; in the winter on the Pacific Coast of California. They breed in some of the interior states in the West.

Look for: A large, almost uniformly gray shorebird with long legs and a long, straight bill. During their breeding months they are more heavily streaked.

Comes to feeders: No.

SPOTTED SANDPIPER

When you'll see them: Year-round.

Where you'll see them: In the northern half of the United States in the spring and summer, southeast and southwest states in the winter.

Look for: Shorebird with very obvious spots on its breast and stomach during the breeding season. Look for its bobbing tail.

Comes to feeders: No.

KILLDEER

When you'll see them: Year-round in the southern half of the United States as well as the Pacific Northwest and Mid-Atlantic, but can be found in the summer throughout the rest of the United States and into a small part of Alaska.

Where you'll see them: Across the United States.

Look for: Large shorebird with brown back, and dark chocolate-hued double necklace.

Comes to feeders: No, but may forage and/or nest in your lawn or field.

SANDERLING

When and where you'll see them: Across all American coast-lines in the winter months (except in Maine), and through the middle of the country and Alaska during migration season.

Look for: A white-and-gray shorebird (in non-breeding, winter plumage), with a black bill and black legs.

Comes to feeders: No.

Both native and introduced for hunting, game and upland birds spend most of their time in dry, upland habitats. Turkey, grouse, and partridges are all game birds.

GREATER ROADRUNNER
When you'll see them: Year-round.

Where you'll see them: The Southwest and into Texas, Louisiana, Oklahoma, and Arkansas.

Look for: A brown-streaked bird with a long tail that runs along the ground.

Comes to feeders: No. Look for them in open, desert habitats.

RUFFED GROUSE
When you'll see them: Year-round.

Where you'll see them: The Northern United States, as well as the Appalachian mountain range and the interior of Alaska.

Look for: Brown, chicken-like bird on the forest floor.

Comes to feeders: No.

SANDHILL CRANE

When you'll see them: Year-round in Florida; during the winter in Texas, parts of Louisiana, parts of Southwestern states and California. They migrate along specific flyways to breed in northern states, Canada, and Alaska.

Where you'll see them: Across the United States during different parts of the year.

Look for: Large gray birds with long legs and red forehead.

Comes to feeders: No.

WILD TURKEY

When you'll see them: Year-round.

Where you'll see them: Across the United States, except Alaska.

Look for: Giant, brown bird walking along the ground, with a bald head.

Comes to feeders: Yes, to corn or birdseed on the ground.

Hummers, as they are sometimes known, are small and stubby, with super sharp, needle-like bills and a fast wingbeat that allows them to hover in place.

RUBY-THROATED HUMMINGBIRD

When you'll see them: Spring and summer.

Where you'll see them: The eastern United States.

Look for: Green backs, pale bellies, and bright-red throats for males; females are green and white.

Comes to feeders: Yes, to sugar-water hummingbird feeders or native flowers.

RUFOUS HUMMINGBIRD

When and where you'll see them: The western United States in spring and summer.

Look for: Males are bright orange with a white chest; females have a more greenish back with rusty patches and a white belly.

Comes to feeders: Yes, to sugar-water hummingbird feeders or native flowers.

ANNA'S HUMMINGBIRD

When and where you'll see them: West Coast states, New Mexico, Arizona. Year-round.

Look for: Males have pink-orange throat and head, while females are more drab, with green-and-white plumage.

Comes to feeders: Yes, to sugar-water hummingbird feeders or native flowers.

BROAD-TAILED HUMMINGBIRD

When and where you'll see them: In the summer months they can be found in habitat patches in Texas, California, Arizona, New Mexico, Nevada, Utah, Idaho, Wyoming, Colorado, and Oregon.

Look for: Green backs and white fronts; males have a red chin, while females have a white chin. In flight, they have white tips on their tail feathers, followed by a stripe of black, then a reddish stripe.

Comes to feeders: Yes, to sugar-water feeders. Planting flowers will also bring them to your yard.

Rare or recovering, these species are threatened or are on the brink of extinction. We must do all we can to protect them and protect the habitat they need to survive and thrive!

CALIFORNIA CONDOR
When you'll see them: Year-round in very specific regions.

Where you'll see them: Parts of California, Nevada, Arizona, and Utah.

Look for: Very large vulture; all black except white patchiness beneath wings.

Comes to feeders: No.

AMERICAN FLAMINGO
When you'll see them: Year-round in very specific regions.

Where you'll see them: Parts of Florida.

Look for: Large pink bird with long legs; large half pink, half black bill.

Comes to feeders: No.

WHOOPING CRANES

When you'll see them: Varies by specific region.

Where you'll see them: There are only small populations of Whooping Cranes left. They live in Canada and move to Texas during migration. Another group flies from Wisconsin to Florida. There are two populations that do not migrate: in Florida and Louisiana.

Look for: Large white bird with long, dark legs and red-and-black patches on head.

Comes to feeders: No.

GOLDEN EAGLE

When you'll see them: In the winter in the eastern half of the United States; year-round in the western half of the United States; migrates through the Northeast; summer in Alaska.

Where you'll see them: Across the United States.

Look for: Very large bird of prey, very dark.

Comes to feeders: No.

REDDISH EGRET

When you'll see them: Year-round where they occur.

Where you'll see them: Gulf Coast states, some areas along the Atlantic Coast of Florida.

Look for: Large wading bird; reddish head and chest, blue-gray back; pink bill with black tip.

Comes to feeders: No.

KIRTLAND'S WARBLER

When and where you'll see them: Parts of Wisconsin and Michigan where they breed in the summer, and along their very specific migration path from these two states to wintering grounds in the Bahamas.

Look for: Dark back and head with broken white eye-ring, some black spotting on flanks.

Comes to feeders: No.

ELF OWL

When and where you'll see them: Parts of the Southwest during the summer breeding season.

Look for: Small owl with speckled brown-and-white back and pale chest and stomach. Bright-yellow-and-black eyes.

Comes to feeders: No.

NēNē, OR HAWAIIAN GOOSE

When and where you'll see them: Hawaii, year-round.

Look for: Black-headed goose with pale neck and brown body.

Comes to feeders: No.

GREEN JAY
When and where you'll see them: Southern tip of Texas, year-round.

Look for: Blue-and-black head, green back, yellow stomach.

Comes to feeders: No.

BLUE-FOOTED BOOBY
When and where you'll see them: Coastal southern California.

Look for: Bright-blue feet.

Comes to feeders: No.

PIPING PLOVER
When and where you'll see them: They nest along inland water bodies in the summer months, or along the northeastern coast. They winter on beaches along the Gulf coast and along the beaches in Southeastern states.

Look for: An orange bill with a black tip; yellow/orange legs.

Comes to feeders: No.

FLORIDA SCRUB-JAY
When and where you'll see them: Florida scrub habitat, year-round.

Look for: Bright-blue head and back, white/silver stomach.

Comes to feeders: No.

GOLDEN-CHEEKED WARBLER
When and where you'll see them: Inland Texas in the summer months.

Look for: A bright-yellow face with a black eye stripe.

Comes to feeders: No.

LUCIFER HUMMINGBIRD
When and where you'll see them: Small parts of the Southwest in the summer months.

Look for: Males have a bright-purple throat.

Comes to feeders: No.

WHITE-TAILED TROPICBIRD

When and where you'll see them: Off the coast near the Dry Tortugas or Hawaii. It is the national bird of Bermuda.

Look for: A very long tail feather.

Comes to feeders: No.

GREATER SAGE GROUSE

When and where you'll see them: Year-round in some parts of the Northwest States, into Colorado, New Mexico, Arizona, and California.

Look for: A large ground bird streaked brown and white. Males have a white chest and black face.

Comes to feeders: No.

How You Can Help Birds

Birding Activites & Projects

How You Can Help Birds

Turn off lights at night so birds don't get disoriented and run into windows. During the day, place Acopian BirdSavers, spaced string, or film over windows to reduce their reflectiveness so birds don't accidentally fly into the glass. You can

work with your town or city on a "lights out" initiative to turn off building lights during migration in the fall and spring. More info: www.audubon.org/lights-out-program

Keep cats indoors. More than 2.5 billion birds are killed by cats each year. The added benefit? Indoor cats are healthier and live longer lives.

Plant native plants instead of lawns. Native plants provide food and shelter for a variety of bird species; by planting them in your backyard, you can watch these beautiful species from the comfort of your home!

Reduce or stop using pesticides in your garden, lawn, and property.

American Robin

Uh oh! Birds can eat plastic accidentally, interfering with their digestion and making them sick. Plastic takes hundreds of years to degrade, so reduce, reuse, and recycle your plastic. Properly dispose of trash so it does not end up in a natural environment.

Tell people how much you love birds! If everyone cares about birds, we can work together to keep them safe now and into the future.

Leave Feathers and Nests Be

BIRD'S NESTS

While it may seem like a fun idea to take a bird's nest home, if there are chicks or eggs inside, it is illegal under the Migratory Bird Treaty Act—even if it's on the ground. It's important to protect nests for future birds to use, so take photos, make sketches, or create your own bird's nest!

FEATHERS

Bird feathers regularly fall out, a process designed to weed out damaged feathers or prepare the bird for changes in breeding plumage. If you find a feather, you can take a photo, sketch it, or admire it, but you probably need to leave it where you found it.

The Migratory Bird Treaty Act was designed to protect birds from hunting, especially for feathers. If you have a feather from birds covered under this law—which is most of them— wildlife officers wouldn't know if you had found it on the ground or if you had hurt the bird to get it. By leaving the feather where you found it, you are helping to protect them!

Banded Birds

Birds are very difficult to study. For one thing, most can fly, which means researchers can't follow them as they grow from chicks to adults and migrate from breeding to wintering grounds and back again. But the more we learn about their life cycles, populations, and movement patterns, the more we can do to protect them.

To work through some of these issues, scientists have used bird bands for decades as a way to track individual birds as they fly from place to place. After receiving a special permit from the U.S. government, these biologists can put specially numbered and colored bands on a bird's legs—just like a bracelet. Because of the unique numbers and colors, when the bird is seen again, we will know exactly which bird we

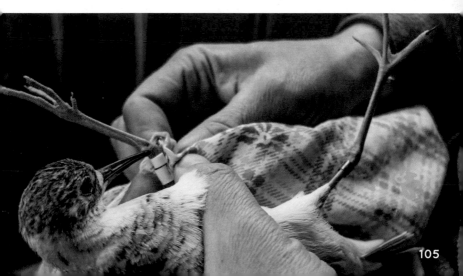

are looking at. By compiling as much of these sightings as possible, scientists begin to understand where birds go after being banded, if they return to the same nesting sites, how long they survive, and so much more.

While you're birding, look closely for these bands. If you see one, take a photo, or note the color and placement of each band: is it above the joint or below  the joint? Are there bands on each leg or only on one leg? Which color belongs with each band? Then submit your sighting to www.reportband.gov. If you're lucky, a biologist will reply with more information about your bird, including its age, where it was banded as a chick, and how many other times this bird has been sighted.

Bird bands are most commonly found on sea and shorebirds, but they can also be spotted on Roseate Spoonbills, songbirds, woodpeckers, vultures, and more!

Blue Jay

Getting More Involved in Birding
WHAT IS A BIG YEAR?

Sometimes, really avid birders decide they want to see
as many birds as possible in a
given area, whether it is their
town, county, state, country,
or even across the whole
world. Mostly for fun, when a
birder commits to seeing as
many birds as possible it is

known as a "Big Year." While many people travel for a
Big Year, you can do your own Big Year in your backyard and local park by paying special attention to bird
species year-round.

COMMUNITY SCIENCE: eBIRD

Birders across the United States and around
the world record their observations
and submit them to eBird, a community science project run by the
Cornell Lab of Ornithology. Available
as a website or phone app, eBird allows individu-
als to collect data on what species of birds they
spot, where they spotted them, and how many they
counted. As of 2021, birders have submitted more
than 100 million observations! The data is used by
researchers and scientists to learn more about

how birds migrate, how climate change affects their populations, and where they live at different times of year. Birders use the app to decide where they should go birding, or where they should look for specific species.

Note: If you record birds in your yard or another place that is private, you can "hide" your observations so people do not see the location. Otherwise, your data is public.

Learn more at ebird.org

Northern Cardinal

THE CHRISTMAS BIRD COUNT

The Christmas Bird Count is the world's oldest community science project. In 1900, Frank Chapman, an early conservationist, suggested that instead of shooting birds as a holiday tradition, people should count them instead.

On that special, inaugural day, 27 birders held 25 Christmas Bird Counts from Canada to California to New England.

Today, Christmas Bird Counts run from mid-December through early January and collect critical data about where birds spend their winters.

To participate, find a Christmas Bird Count happening near you using the website below, and join the fun! New birders can participate, and they are encouraged to join a group that has at least one experienced birder as well.

Each Christmas Bird Count is done within a 15-mile-wide circle, with pre-determined routes. Each bird spotted or heard is counted.

Learn more at www.audubon.org/conservation/join-christmas-bird-count

GLOBAL BIG DAY

As a celebration of birding, and a way to give scientists a snapshot of birdlife around the world on a single day, birders come together each year for the Global Big Day. This event draws thousands of people every year, including more than 50,000 in 2020!

Andean Condor

People in almost 200 countries looked for birds, for a total of 120,000+ checklists. That is amazing!

Participating is easy. Bird for at least 10 minutes on the designated day, wherever you choose. Enter your checklist on eBird (you will need an eBird account), and watch what other people are seeing near you or across the Earth.

Learn more at: https://ebird.org/globalbigday

GREAT BACKYARD BIRD COUNT

Members and supporters of the National Audubon Society, the Cornell Lab of Ornithology, and Birds Canada flock together to count birds over a four-day period, usually in late winter. All the observations taken together create a "snap-shot" of bird numbers, which scientists can use not

only to determine where birds live and feed in the winter, but also to compare and contrast to past years to see how bird populations are changing over time.

Once birders sign up, they only have to count birds for 15 minutes to participate— though they can bird for as long or as often as they wish to over the multi-day count window. Observations are tracked on eBird.

Mountain Chickadee

Learn more:
www.birdcount.org/

PLANNING A BIRDING ROAD TRIP

You've mastered all the bird species in your back-yard—that's great! Now it's time to plan a birding road trip with a trusted adult.

1) **Decide what kinds of birds you want to see.**
   Do they require a specific habitat you will have to find? For example, if you live in a suburban neighborhood, but really want to spot seabirds and shorebirds, you'll have to venture to a beach or an estuary.

2) **Make a list of locations** that have that specific bird or birds. Use the mapping tools on ebird.org or on the eBird app to discover where others have been seeing these birds. You will have to visit public lands that are open to visitors, such as parks, wildlife management areas, public beaches, wildlife refuges, or greenways.

   Don't have a specific bird or group of birds in mind? That's no problem! eBird can also help you identify birding hotspots, where other bird enthusiasts have found lots of birds in one place.

3) **Plot the places you want to see** on a digital or paper map to make sure you can see them all in one day, or in the days you have allotted to your birding road trip. Smaller parks can be visited in an hour or two, but large areas may need a full day of exploration. If you're unsure, call the park rangers or land managers—they are happy to help!

   Make sure you look up when the parks or natural areas are open, if they require a fee, and what their trails systems look like. Download maps or print them ahead of time. Unless you have special permission from the owner, you cannot bird on private property, so avoid those areas.

4) **Decide how you will keep track of your list**, or if you want to use a list at all. Do you prefer keeping track of birds in the eBird app or website? Or will you want to bring a nature notebook along?

5) **Download or bring a field guide** to help identify new birds. A camera can help by taking photos to compare to a digital or in-print field guide later.

6) **Think about the conditions at each site.** You will definitely need water and comfortable walking shoes, but do you also need hiking boots or mud boots? Do you need a rain jacket? Will you be gone long enough to need snacks or a packed meal? Do you need bugspray? Figuring out the gear and supplies you need the day before will keep you safe during your road trip.

7) **Have fun!** Birding road trips are great ways to spend time with friends and family, while exploring the natural world.

State Birds

Did you know that each of the 50 states has a state bird? Voted on by state legislators, each official bird symbolizes what elected officials feel is important for their states. Some birds are more popular than others—the Northern Cardinal is the state bird for seven states!

ALABAMA
Northern Flicker

ALASKA
Willow Ptarmigan

ARIZONA
Cactus Wren

ARKANSAS
Northern Mockingbird

CALIFORNIA
California Quail

COLORADO
Lark Bunting

CONNECTICUT
American Robin

WASHINGTON DC
Wood Thrush

DELAWARE
Delaware Blue Hen

FLORIDA
Northern Mockingbird

GEORGIA
Brown Thrasher

HAWAII
NēNē

IDAHO
Mountain Bluebird

ILLINOIS
Northern Cardinal

INDIANA
Northern Cardinal

IOWA
American
Goldfinch

KANSAS
Western
Meadowlark

KENTUCKY
Northern Cardinal

LOUISIANA
Brown Pelican

MAINE
Black-capped
Chickadee

MARYLAND
Baltimore Oriole

MASSACHUSETTS
Black-capped
Chickadee

MICHIGAN
American Robin

MINNESOTA
Common Loon

MISSISSIPPI
Northern
Mockingbird

MISSOURI
Eastern Bluebird

MONTANA
Western
Meadowlark

NEBRASKA
Western
Meadowlark

NEVADA
Mountain Bluebird

NEW HAMPSHIRE
Purple Finch

NEW JERSEY
American Goldfinch

NEW MEXICO
Greater Roadrunner

NEW YORK
Eastern Bluebird

NORTH CAROLINA
Northern Cardinal

NORTH DAKOTA
Western Meadowlark

OHIO
Northern Cardinal

OKLAHOMA
Scissor-tailed Flycatcher

OREGON
Western Meadowlark

PENNSYLVANIA
Ruffed Grouse

RHODE ISLAND
Rhode Island Red

SOUTH CAROLINA
Carolina Wren

SOUTH DAKOTA
Ring-necked Pheasant

TENNESSEE
Northern Mockingbird

TEXAS
Northern Mockingbird

UTAH
California Gull

VERMONT
Hermit Thrush

VIRGINIA
Northern Cardinal

WASHINGTON
American
Goldfinch

WEST VIRGINIA
Northern Cardinal

WISCONSIN
American Robin

WYOMING
Western
Meadowlark

Birding Activities & Projects
KEEP A NATURE JOURNAL

Keeping a nature journal is the best way to truly hone your observation skills and keep your notes safe year after year.

There are many ways to keep a nature journal, and you can choose which method works best for you. If you're not an artist, that's okay! The process of observing and recording what you see is more important than the final product.

1) **Keep lists and take notes.** Each time you head to a natural area or observe your backyard, what do you see? Note the time of day, the weather, and which birds you spot. Take some notes on what the birds are doing. Are they feeding? Flying? Nesting? Make sure you include the date, so you can look back on which birds are easy to see during different seasons.

2) Make sketches. Sketching is one of the best ways to learn field marks. What do the birds look like when they're perched in the tree? What about when they are flying? What colors can you see from far away, and which are more obvious when the birds can be seen close-up? Sketch the same birds over and over to get a feel for how they change from season to season, or seek new species every time.

3) Take photographs. Use photographs to keep a digital nature journal, or print out the images and paste them into a notebook, writing in the margins about what you observed while photographing the birds.

Your observations don't have to be limited to birds—take notes and make sketches of everything you see, including trees, flowers, mushrooms, insects, and more!

HOW TO SKETCH BIRDS

To get the hang of sketching birds, look specifically at what shapes make up their general body and head silhouette. Is It a series of circles? Or spheres attached to curved lines or rectangles? Start with the shapes first, then gradually fill in the details as you keep going.

Once you have the general outline, start filling in different feather shades, starting with the darkest and working towards the lightest areas. Using a pencil is perfect, since you don't have to worry about plumage colors (at least for today).

Use photographs to help you, either ones you take yourself or online. As you get better at sketching, take your pencils into the field and adorn your nature journal with bird pictures!

To view additional sketching lessons with famed bird artist David Sibley, visit: www.audubon.org/magazine/summer-2020/learn-draw-birds-david-sibley

HOW TO ATTRACT HUMMINGBIRDS TO YOUR YARD —THE NATURAL WAY

While you can buy special hummingbird feeders that drip a steady supply of sugar-water to these buzzing birds, there are many natural ways to attract these special species to your yard.

1) **Use red.** Hummingbirds love the color red, so plant red flowers or tie red ribbons to plants or outdoor furniture. Avoid using red dye in your hummingbird mixes: it's bad for the birds.

2) **Plant native species** with bright colors and tubular shapes. Depending on where you live, try bee balm, cardinal flower, zinnias, salvias, and more!

3) **Plant tall shrubs** or trees so hummingbirds have areas to perch as well as feed.

MAKE YOUR YARD BIRD-FRIENDLY

Do bright-green lawns help native bird species? Not really. Birds are attracted to trees, bushes, and native flowers, which they rely on to host the insects and seeds they need to eat to survive (and hummingbirds need flowers!). The best way to bring birds to your yard is to plant native plants.

Where to Start

When you start from a lawn, it can be difficult to choose a place to begin. Don't worry! Use websites like www.audubon.org/native-plants to find out which wildflowers and plants are native to your area, and stop by native plant nurseries to talk to expert staff about which species might survive in your backyard's unique mix of sun and shade. Start with potted plants if that seems more manageable!

Don't forget a water source. Whether it's a bird bath or a small fountain, water lets birds both bathe and drink. Make sure it stays clean!

What to Avoid

Pesticides and herbicides not only harm the very insects you're hoping to attract to your yard, but they can also hurt the birds themselves. What about mosquitoes? Good question! Keep standing water away from your yard, and install a bubbler in your bird bath to keep these bugs from laying eggs in the still water.

Leave Out Nest-making Materials in Spring

One of the best parts of spring and early summer? Bird nesting! To encourage birds to make nests in your yard or neighborhood, you can put out nest-making materials. However, it's important to put out the right materials to keep both adult birds and chicks safe throughout the breeding season.

Nest materials should be natural, as well as pesticide and dye free. While many like to leave out yarn, it is important to note that most yarn sold in large stores is actually made of plastic, and not good to have in bird's nests. Do not leave out any material made from plastic, metal, or lint.

It's much better to use the soft, fluffy plant parts you find in natural areas near where you live, including cattails or milkweed. If you do have access to 100% wool or sheep fleece, you can use that as well.

Place the material in a tree nook or hang it from your bird feeders, then see which birds arrive to take some material home with them!

Make a Recipe to Feed to Birds

If you get creative, you can feed birds a lot more than birdseed! Making your own bird food is a fun way to attract the birds you want to see.

Here are two options, though there are lots of others:

DO-IT-YOURSELF BIRDSEED MIX

A lot of birdseed mixes aren't very good. Often, they have lots of filler seeds, such as milo (a small brown, round seed) instead of black-oil sunflower seed, which is the best seed around.

To avoid this problem, make your own! Buy some black-oil sunflower seed, and use it as your base, then add other seeds to it. Here's a mix that works well for platform feeders. All of the ingredients are usually available at garden centers or home-improvement stores.

4 cups black-oil sunflower seeds

1 cup peanut chips

1 cup cracked corn

Mix it all together, and place it on a hanging bird feeder. Feel free to get creative by adding in sliced apples or plums.

A SIMPLE PEANUT BUTTER BIRDSEED FEEDER

What you'll need

Pine cones

Peanut butter

Black-oil sunflower seeds or
a birdseed mix

Some string

This tried-and-true recipe really
works. First, you'll need to collect some pine cones. Then mix
the peanut butter and sunflower
seeds in a bowl. Next, take the pine
cones and push them into the peanut butter-seed
mix, turning them to cover. After that, simply tie some
string to the top of the pine cone and hang it from a
tree. You can do this as many times as you'd like.

If you don't have any pine cones available, you can
simply mix all of the ingredients together and then
"paint" or smear it onto tree bark.

SET UP A WINDOW FEEDER

When you're first learning to identify bird species, it's
helpful to get an up-close look. But how to do it without scaring the birds away? Simple: a window feeder!

Pick a room in your house where you can comfort-
ably watch your backyard birds. Window feeders use
suction cups to attach to the outside of your window

and use a mirror-like layer between the food and the window. Put simply: you can see them, but they can't see you! Take notes and make sketches so you can remember which birds show up each day.

BIRD NEST CAMS

Don't want to put up a window feeder? No problem! Bird organizations across the country have set up bird's nest cams literally inside the nests of a variety of bird species, from owls to hawks to puffins. You can take a peek anytime you want! For a list, visit: www.allaboutbirds.org/cams/

MAKE YOUR WINDOWS SAFER FOR BIRDS

Hundreds of millions of birds are killed or injured each year when they accidentally fly into windows, often because they saw a reflection of nearby plants or the sky and thought it was a safe place to fly. Such collisions are often fatal, and they are a constant problem.

There are a few simple steps you can take to help:

- Close your blinds or curtains, as this will make the window look more like a barrier. This is very important at night, when a lit-up room might seem like a welcoming place for a bird to fly.

- Turn off lights at night, especially during migration.

- When placing bird feeders, either keep them well away from a window (more than 20 feet) or keep them very close to a window (on the window, via suction cups or a just few feet away). (Even if a bird flies into a window from a close-by feeder, it won't have enough distance to accelerate enough to cause serious injury.)

- A number of "scare tapes" for windows are available and they can be effective.

- Placing ribbons, pinwheels, and other moving accessories in front of windows can scare birds away.

- Keep plants away from windows, as birds often mistake them as a continuation of the natural scenery.

Recommended Reading

Carson, Rachel. *Silent Spring (50th Anniversary Edition)*. New York: Houghton Mifflin, 2002.

Daniels, Jaret. *Native Plant Gardening for Birds, Bees & Butterflies: Midwest*. Cambridge: MN: Adventure Publications, 2020.

Geuder, Jenny deFouw. *Drawn to Birds: A Naturalist's Sketchbook*. Cambridge: MN: Adventure Publications, 2022.

Miller, George Oxford. *Native Plant Gardening for Birds, Bees & Butterflies: Southern California*. Cambridge, MN: Adventure Publications, 2022.

Porter, Adele. *Homemade Bird Food: 26 Fun & Easy Recipes to Feed Backyard Birds*. Cambridge: MN: Adventure Publications, 2020.

Sibley, David Allen. The Sibley Guide to North American Birds, 2nd Edition. New York: Knopf, 2014.

Stiteler, Sharon. *City Birds, Country Birds: How Anyone Can Attract Birds to Their Feeder*. Cambridge: MN: Adventure Publications, 2008.

Tekiela, Stan. *Bird Nests: Amazingly Ingenious and Intricate*. Cambridge: MN: Adventure Publications, 2015.

Tekiela, Stan. *Feathers: A Beautiful Look at a Bird's Most Unique Feature*. Cambridge: MN: Adventure Publications, 2014.

Tekiela, Stan. *Hummingbirds: Marvels of the Bird World*. Cambridge: MN: Adventure Publications, 2022.

Glossary

Carrion an animal that has died and is eaten by another animal.

Climate change The burning of fossil fuels releases greenhouse gases, which in turn heats the earth and raises global temperatures. The rising temperatures change the climate across the globe in different ways.

Crest Birds have a crest when they can move the feathers on their heads up and down. Examples: Northern Cardinals and Blue Jays.

Extinct When all members of a species die out.

Field Marks The colors, shapes, and sizes of birds that help you identify one bird from another.

Irruption When birds that usually only migrate short distances or don't migrate at all move very far from their normal range, usually in search of food or territory.

Life Bird or "Lifer" The first time you personally see a species for the first time.

Metabolism The rate at which a bird's body changes food into energy.

Migration When some bird species move from a wintering range to a breeding range, usually in search of more food or nesting resources. Spring and fall are the migration seasons.

Non-native A species that was introduced to a new area, where it historically did not live.

Plumage The feathers that cover a bird's body.

Range Where a bird lives.

Spark Bird The bird that first made you fall in love with bird-watching.

Year List The number of bird species you see within one calendar year.

Northern Parula

Your Birding Life List

SPECIES	DATE	SIGHTING NOTES (location, habitat, bird activity)

SPECIES	DATE	SIGHTING NOTES (location, habitat, bird activity)

SPECIES	DATE	SIGHTING NOTES (location, habitat, bird activity)

Photo credits, *continued from page 2*

Images used under license from Shutterstock.com:
A Zargar: 28 (right); a454: 112; Adrian Eugen Ciobaniuc: 85 (top); Agami Photo Agency: 72 (top), 73 (top), 86 (bottom), 98 (bottom), 114 (HI & WA DC); Agnieszka Bacal: 18 (middle), 21 (top), 88 (bottom), 116 (PA); Alan B. Schroeder: 115 (MO); Alejo Miranda: 14; Aleksandr Ozerov: 16 (chicks); Alexey Stlop: 9 (robin eggs); alexkich: 50; Alexonline: 9 (bones illustration); all_about_people: 48; Andrea J Smith: 17 (egg); Archaeopteryx Tours: 116 (SC); Ariene Studio: 116 (Rhode Island); Barb Elkin: 83 (left); Barmalini: 122 (top); Bartow Photography: 31 (top); Beekeepx: 102 (top); benpassarelli: 87 (bottom); Bildagentur Zoonar GmbH: 62 (bottom left), 123; Blue Planet Studio: 84 (top); BlueRingMedia: 21 (middle); Bonnie Taylor Barry: 20 (bottom left), 56 (top), 60 (top), 62 (top right), 64 (top), 115 (IL, IN & KY), 116 (NC & OH), 117 (VA), 122 (bottom), 129; Brent Simon: 76 (top); Brian A Wolf: 87 (top), 92 (top); Brian E Kushner: 28 (middle); Brian Lasenby: 65 (middle), 71 (middle), 78 (bottom), 81 (bottom left), 82 (bottom right), 94 (top), 115 (LA), 116 (NJ); brizmaker: 127; Byron Layton: 27 (bottom); Capitan Crizelini: 75 (bottom); Carrie Olson: 81 (top right); Catcher of Light, Inc.: 19 (top right); Chanonry: 9 (puffin); Charlotte Payne: 125; Chiyacat: 17 (nesting), 110 (bottom); Chris Hill: 74 (bottom); Christian Weber: 95 (bottom); Dan Thornberg: 36 (top); Danita Delimont: 58 (bottom), 63 (top right), 108, 111; Dave Allen Photography: 41 (top); David Spates: 115 (MT); David Thyberg: 99 (top); Debra Anderson: 57 (top); Denisa Mikesova: 29 (bottom); Dennis W Donohue: 116 (NM); Double Brow Imagery: 69 (top), 116 (NV); Dr. Alan Lipkin: 75 (middle); Drakuliren: 12 (top); DrPospisil: 33 (bottom); Eivor Kuchta: 28 (left), 63 (bottom left), 68 (top); Ekatsyerina Kostsina: 52; EM Arts: 124; F.Rubino: 11 (crocodile); f11photo: 34 (bottom); Feng Yu: 65 (bottom); Fiona M. Donnelly: 90 (top), 114 (AL); FotoRequest: 32 (bottom), 59 (bottom), 65 (top), 74 (top); Frode Jacobsen: 22, 29 (top), 75 (top), 130; George Highlands: 16 (eggs); Gerald A. DeBoer: 17 (adult), 116 (TN); GERMANZEILER: 82 (top right); Glass and Nature: 6, 72 (bottom); Grafko: 93 (bottom); gregg williams: 58 (top); Harry Collins Photography: 23 (right), 42; Heather L. Hubbard: 18 (bottom); Igor Pushkarev: 92 (bottom); ilkah: 64 (bottom); J. Breedlove: 106 (bands); J. Omar Hanse: 73 (bottom); Jack Bell Photography: 71 (bottom), 115 (KS); James Lawson: 56 (bottom); Janick C: 70 (bottom); Jeff Grabert: 24 (top); Jeff Rzepka: 94 (bottom); Jeff W. Jarrett: 68 (bottom); Jemny: 88 (top); Jeremy Christensen: 35 (bottom); JGA: 1 (birdhouse), 3 (birdhouse); Jim Cumming: 26, 106 (blue jay), 115 (MN); Jim Nelson: 80 (top); Joe Ferrer: 93 (top); Joe McDonald: 114 (AR); Joel Trick: 115 (MD); John Fader: 117 (WA); Jordan Feeg: 19 (bottom left); Josef Hanus: 34 (top); Juris Vigulis: 80 (bottom); Justin Henke: 55 (top); Kalyanby: 105; Karyn Honor: 79 (top); Katelyn Luff: 116 (OR); Ken Griffiths: 44; Keneva Photography: 23 (left), 31 (bottom), 90 (bottom), 91 (top); Kent Raney: 91 (bottom); Kerry Hargrove: 117 (WY); Klahan: 1 (nest), 3 (nest); kriangkrainetnangrong: 49; Kristi Blokhin: 33 (top), 126; Kristin Howell: 30 (bottom); Krumpelman Photography: 76 (bottom); LeQuangN-hut: 31 (middle); Lidia fotografie: 116 (ND); Lisa Holder: 115 (IA); little birdie: 104; Lori Skelton: 43; LorraineHudgins: 45; lunamarina: 114 (DE); M. Leonard Photography: 115 (NE); Maridav: 113; MarkBrandon: 11 (top); Mark C. Morris: 86 (top); Martin Mecnarowski: 110 (top); Martin Pelanek: 27 (top); 67 (bottom); Mati Kose: 19 (middle right); Matthew Winks: 67 (middle); Melinda Fawver: 8 (bottom); 71 (top); Michael Armentrout: 98 (top); Michael Chatt: 89 (top); Michael Siluk: 61 (top); Michal Dobes: 11 (turtles); Mike Truchon: 11 (birds), 121; Mircea Costina: 70 (top); Monika Wilk Photo: 10; MTKhaled mahmud: 30 (top), 115 (ID); Nasky: 13, 15 (both); Natalia Kuzmina: 67 (top), 116 (OK); Nelson Sirlin: 37, 61, 14 (AZ); Nick Bossenbroek: 77 (bottom); Nick Pecker: 117 (UT); Panaiotidi: 38; Panumas Yanuthai: 118; Patricia Stamp: 57 (bottom); Paul Reeves Photography: 18 (top), 59 (top), 117 (WI); Paul Roedding: 62 (top left); Paul Tessier: 89 (bottom); Photo Spirit: 117 (VT); Piotr Krzeslak: 116 (SD); Potapov Alexander: 20 (egg); PUGUH YUDHA: 9 (great egret); R.C. Bennett: 114 (GA); R_Branham: 103; Ramona Edwards: 17 (juvenile); Randy G. Lubischer: 97 (top); Raul Baena: 60 (bottom); Raul Baena: 114 (Florida); rck_953: 116 (TX); Reimar: 102 (bottom); Ricardo Reitmeyer: 35 (top); Robert Adami: 85 (bottom); Romeo Andrei Cana: 63 (top left); RT Images: 77 (top); RudiErnst: 83 (right); Rud-mer Zwerver: 11 (mammals); Sambulov Yevgeniy: 46; samuelsylf: 5; sandymsj: 79 (bottom); Sarah Tee: 115 (ME); sebartz: 115 (MA); Serhiy Kozodavov: 11 (snake); silentwings_M_Ghosh:

Page 39 – Carolina Parakeet, John J. Audubon (public domain) https://en.wikipedia.org/wiki/Carolina_parakeet#/media/File:AudubonCarolinaParakeet2.jpg

Page 39 – Martha, Smithsonian Institution (public domain) https://www.si.edu/object/passenger-pigeon-martha-division-birds-exhibit-natural-history-building:siris_arc_402404

Page 39 – Ivory-billed Woodpecker, John J. Audubon (public domain) https://en.wikipedia.org/wiki/Ivory-billed_woodpecker#/media/File:Campephilus_principalisAWP066AA2.jpg

Page 39 – Great Auk, Jonn J. Audubon (public domain) https://en.wikipedia.org/wiki/Great_auk#/media/File:Keulemans-GreatAuk.jpg

Page 39 – Eskimo Curlew, Archibald Thorburn (public domain) https://en.wikipedia.org/wiki/Eskimo_curlew#/media/File:Numenius_borealis.jpg

Page 40 - Omaha Daily Bee, October 10, 1915, via chroniclingamerica.loc.gov

Page 41 - The Minneapolis Journal, January 25, 1904, via chroniclingamerica.loc.gov

Page 47 - climate map & colorbar, NOAA and Climate.gov

Page 62 - Mexican Chickadee, Poecile sclateri, Barfoot, Cave Creek Arizona by Bettina Arrigoni, licensed via a Creative Commons 2.0 Attribution Generic license (https://creativecommons.org/licenses/by/2.0/); original image available here: https://www.flickr.com/photos/barrigoni/21626198892/

About the Author

Erika Zambello is a writer, naturalist, and communications specialist. After receiving a Master's Degree in Environmental Management from Duke University, where she specialized in Ecosystem Science and Conservation, she traveled across the United States visiting important science and naturalist sites for the Florida Park Service, the Long Term Ecological Research Network, National Parks Traveler, NOAA, and more. Her work has appeared in *BirdWatching Daily, Backpacker, National Geographic Adventure, National Parks Traveler, Guy Harvey Magazine, Florida Sportsman,* and *Coastal Angler.* She is the author of *Backyard Science & Discovery Workbook: South* and *Coastal Life of the Atlantic and Gulf Coasts.* When she is not working, she is exploring near her home in North Florida, looking for native bird species. She lives in Tallahassee with her husband, kid, and two cats.